Eine feste Burg in der ich mich verstecken kann!

A fort for me to hide inside!

Ein Segel, das im Winde flappt,

A ship's sails flapping in the air,

Eine Schmusedecke, die mich tröstet wenn Mama nicht da ist.

A comforter when she's not there.

Ein Beduinenzelt,

A bedouin tent,

Ein Hochzeitssari,

A wedding sari,

Ein Tischtuch für mein Picknick.

A cloth for my tea party.

Der Umhang einer Stammeskönigin,

A warrior queen's cloak,

Ein Reisesack für die Nomaden,

A nomad's baggage,

Eine Decke unter der ich schlafen kann!

A blanket when I need a rest!

Aber Mamas Kopf zu bedecken
als Zeichen ihres Glaubens,
das ist, wozu dieses Kopftuch
wirklich da ist.

But covering my mum
as part of her faith
Is what the hijaab does best.

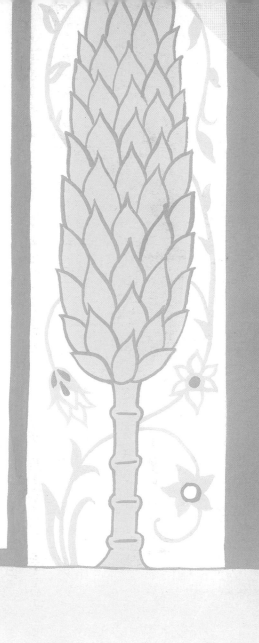

Bismillahir-Rahmanir-Raheem

For the daughters of Islam, past, present and future

N.B.R.

For Saarah, Farheen & Rayaan

N.M.

The Swirling Hijaab is one of many sound enabled books.
Touch the circle with TalkingPEN for a list of the other titles.

First published in 2002 Mantra Lingua Ltd
Global House, 303 Ballards Lane, London N12 8NP
www.mantralingua.com

A CIP record for this book is available from the British Library